T0057573

THE
WAY
OF
THE
EARTH

Also by Matthew Shenoda

Bearden's Odyssey
(edited with Kwame Dawes)

Tahrir Suite

Seasons of Lotus, Seasons of Bone

Somewhere Else

THE
WAY
OF
THE
EARTH

POEMS

MATTHEW SHENODA

TriQuarterly Books / Northwestern University Press
Evanston, Illinois

TriQuarterly Books
Northwestern University Press
www.nupress.northwestern.edu

Copyright © 2022 by Northwestern University. Published 2022 by TriQuarterly
Books / Northwestern University Press. All rights reserved.

Printed in the United States of America

10   9   8   7   6   5   4   3   2   1

Library of Congress Cataloging-in-Publication Data

Names: Shenoda, Matthew, author.
Title: The way of the Earth : poems / Matthew Shenoda.
Description: Evanston : TriQuarterly Books/Northwestern University Press, 2022.
Identifiers: LCCN 2022020584 | ISBN 9780810145665 (paperback) | ISBN
    9780810145672 (ebook)
Subjects: LCGFT: Poetry.
Classification: LCC PS3619.H4538 W39 2023 | DDC 811/.6—dc23/
    eng/20220427
LC record available at https://lccn.loc.gov/2022020584

For Dimyana, Kyrillos, and Pishoy,
the bearers of our name, antecedent, and song.

For Christina, my unabridged spirit.

For Pops and Minreet, always.

For Mama, Anthony, Maryann, Makarios, and Seraphim.

We are hard pressed on every side, but not crushed; perplexed, but not in despair; persecuted, but not abandoned; struck down, but not destroyed.

—2 Corinthians 4:8–9

So far away from where it's happening
you think you found a place of peace
just to find it's happening everywhere,
it's happening here, there, and
everywhere.

—Bob Marley

CONTENTS

Prelude

1

Time   *3*

Glint   *4*

Sleep   *6*

Traces   *8*

Fire   *9*

To Be Carried by Air   *11*

Evolution   *12*

Loss   *13*

Still   *15*

Oil and Myrrh   *16*

Crossing Over   *18*

Midday Sun   *19*

The Edge Is the End of the Beginning   *21*

2

Coastal   *27*

Succession   *29*

Local   *31*

Canto for Pasadena   *32*

In the "Post-Conflict" Nation   *34*

Our Returning   36

Song of the Dispersed   37

Thaw   39

Work   40

Who Feels It, Knows It   42

Wild   46

Unknowing   48

Glimpse   49

Seeing   51

Refuge   53

An Afternoon in July   55

Rock Head   57

The Unlearning   59

Revelation: Africa: Diaspora   61

Acknowledgments   63

And they said to the elder,
firm in his beliefs:

"The whole world is
against you!"

To which he replied:

"And I am against
the whole world!"

1

TIME

Time never goes backwards,
but the imagination must.

In the small grooves of a pinewood floor
the recesses of footsteps
worn by the pressures of a human life.

Light reflected in the contours
sings back the gait of a man once held

pacing in anticipation of new life
the way a weighty branch might split a trunk,
expose the textures of smooth and rough.

He could never quite recall who stole his ambition,
whether cross-continental amnesia
or the wearing of a body
tested by the trials of a circumspect host

the way one might expect relief from the heat,
shelter, a gesture of human kindness
extended through an ancient notion of
bread and oil,
a table for the passerby.

GLINT

How often we have spoken
of the quality of light

The way the fern holds
drops of rain

Each encompassing the world around it
magnified like fire

Consuming the breach of desire
a branch reaching for another

A root made manifest
in the expanse of sky

The way her hand dips slowly
into the space of another.

How do we call ourselves by names
other than our own?

How do we walk
without feeling our flesh?

The rough facade of a brick building
or the considered touch of another's hand

Our palms can hold within them
all the beauty we have come to know.

The whole of the world
was never ours to have

But that which our palms can touch
that space we hold between each hand

That is our earth and our sun
our reminder that we are still alive.

SLEEP

With the door cracked open
a mist of rain crossed the threshold
and entered the room.

His hand reaching
a gentle stroke on his face,
the recognition of kin.

Lashes made of ancient thread
capture the breath of his brother
and flutter in the seed of his sleep.

We make our bread from the warmth
that seeks us,
rekindle the coals of our desires.

I remember the winding mountain roads,
the green of earth from a back seat
the swaying motion of childhood memory.

Dry earth, abundant
hills that stretched the length of an imagination
made fire by the kindling of sleep.

And now, in this moment,
the egrets of the salt marshes
making room for the currents of memory.

I learned from my father,
long before I ever understood
what it meant to be a person on this earth

how one lives for moments that make our compass clear,
give us enough view to see the next moment,
and cultivate its gifts.

The rise and fall of their chests
a steadiness of sound
cultivating strength for the days to come.

TRACES

In the hard shadow of the moon
when the recesses of light have gone
and the faint red of the hawk's shoulder has disappeared from the sky
in the growing pulse of the praying mantis
when the city has come into its own new light
it is here where I often remember:

the weaving of ocean vines
the trails of history, cemented by touch
the small ridged blossom of the cowrie shell
the indigo dye made radiant by the seller's basket.

The way the long grass
emerges at the shore.
Something of that meeting.

These are memories both distant and near
traces of them lived and felt
laughing in the company of the ones who came
holding the silence of the moment, as we stare
with wonder, at the bubbling ruptures of a painter's canvas,
pull, with care, the clinging skin of a stubborn fruit.

I recall these moments
not from the grand gesture
of a thing once known,
but from a small place,
the place where my child's hand
is hidden warmly inside my own.

FIRE

The hills here have always been a mercy
a procession of relief, stretching into an untenable sun.

Chaparral cut by the dusted stamp of a rabbit's foot
everything alive in the saline air.

We live at once in the silhouette of such things
even when blinded,

we are always in the shadow
of something.

Embers of fires
the black pinions floating toward earth.

When the fires struck we watched the miles
stretch across the Pacific

knowing that the hard earth could call for rain
that the sky could root itself like an ancient umbilical.

Unseen lightning
the twin of a new beginning.

When the earth spoke black
we knew a new day was coming

we knew we would not be devoured
until our time had come.

When I was young, we had an olive tree in the yard
a blanket beneath its branches

we would shake the trunk
until the sky rained black

savor the salted pluck
and seed the earth with our spent desires.

TO BE CARRIED BY AIR

The leaves of the trees expended
like the last breath of a seabird
careening for a final plunge.

The air of the sea
a reminder of the easy days
before the belabored pull from deep inside
before a sickness made from time and neglect.

When the kits emerge from the den
do they know that the world has changed—
new to them, but from before them?

I labor in my own mind and toil
a tumbler of coffee beside me,
each drip like a gentle pine bough
caressing the bark of my throat.

In a place so much closer to "home"
worn fingers pick the bean
that makes its way
across untold thresholds.

Black cowrie
a currency of scent and steam.

With the window cracked open
the salt air of the sea
and the lifting floral of my cup,
a coalescence,
not unlike that of the journeys
that brought us here.

EVOLUTION

A child spins a top
and watches it topple from the edge of a table.

All the ways of knowing
have never added up to a single whole.

A bird call
is a bird call.
Whether grouse or hawk
it is not human
and neither can we fly.

Conclude what you will
but location seems central
to understanding.

The arch of the ark
that put us all here.

And a past, never past
the testimony
of rock
of arrow
of sword
of bullet

the condition of a stagnant heart.

LOSS

He took from the bowl
rice steaming
the scent of spices
and the heat of the stove still warming the room.

It was imagined,
this thing
this memory
triggered by scent
an unmoored ship on a saline horizon.

It took him into wonder
but not the kind of playful wonder
a child might recount.

It took him inside himself
not unlike the way the edge of a knife
works under the delicate skin of fruit.

And in these moments he would breathe,
recount the breath she struggled for.

Maybe possibility has always been a part of our breath—
that thing that we exhale
into the cool air of an unknown future.

Like the generosity of fire and water.

Oxygen.

Maybe in the heart of a fallible man
lies honesty.

A different kind of oxygen,

an accelerant

a burning thing
like the peppers
swirling in his mouth.

STILL

At a sacrosanct river's edge
ideation becomes a torn recollection.

As the elder says,
"Knowledge of fire
does not warm the body."

And all that we think we know
flakes like dirt to expose stone.

And here we begin again.

Running our hands on the smooth surface
collecting dust older than our thoughts could ever be.

Imagine lightning.
Imagine rain.
Imagine quiet,
strung with bits of wind.

Imagine the tender ripple
of foliage meeting water.

Imagine the anticipation of creation
still, in welcome,
open, awaiting our touch
running our hands on the smooth of her surface.

————

The quote comes from Saint Maximus the Confessor.

OIL AND MYRRH
for Minreet

1

There is no simplicity
in the motives of another man

How she'd never hear the sound of her own humming

Could not contemplate the slices
of an orange, of rind & flesh

Understand earth
through the soles of her feet

There would be music
made only from machines
the monotone piercing
an electronic origination
not from the hands of humans
or the skins of animals

And the touch of wires and tubes
would impress themselves deeper
than the touch of fingers
save one thumb
slick with oil and myrrh
In the name of the Father . . .

2

We tell ourselves differently
but there are only two worlds

One inhabited by the hubris of men
the other of spirit and ancestor
of those who find their wisdom beyond a grave.

3

She could not take the same breath we take
to re-create creation in the simple wind of her chest

Men make machines
so they can live on
but life is something altogether different

To taste on the tongue
is a gateway
a communion
an unearthly understanding

A rhythm steadied for a song
that tells the world
the sun sets in the east.

CROSSING OVER

I stole from the bark of my own desires
depleted that rough which shields our insides
and stood in testament of what's to come.

Each of us gets called
one way or another.

Open like the river
eroding with each storm.
Dubious light
illuminating the banks to the other side

the way water might crack
as it meets the earth;
repetitive shudder
from an unseen source.

This too is a kind of grace
an unmasking, a view of what's to come.

> To place each rock in the garden
> with intention,
> that someday it may be a resting post
> for the weary.

It doesn't take all of what we often think.
A slight breeze
a quiet moment
a clear view of the other side.

MIDDAY SUN

Idling at the port
faded green like the metallic back
of an insect bathed in light.

A slow rumble, laden with pots and nets
the bow facing west
pushing for the far horizon.

We decorate our homes with words
return the burden of our forgetting
like the bobbing head of a shore bird

the rolling line of a swell
moving to the jagged edge
of a deep-sea bass line.

Visceral is the moment of memory
the way I moved like a creature, wings tucked in,
floating up the coast of my childhood.

Week after week I returned to see my dying father
his final days in the geography of my childhood
so far from his own.

The hills painted with the shadows of walks we long took
before time moved us across the palimpsest of memory
before returning, before the compass grew roots.

The last time he pulled me close with his words
he told me of the future I would live
breathed into me, the way someone breathed into him

the way the fishing nets in that not too distant sea
linked, one loop to another,
each held by the strength of the one before it.

THE EDGE IS THE END OF THE BEGINNING
for Minreet

1

I have come from the virtue of the mountaintop
the lampwick, not the light
descending down switchbacks
scent of dampness & tree bark
pine needles scattered at my feet
like sand parted by weight.

When I round the corner to the next vista
full of mist & light
I will find an understanding
wrapped in the haze of a calling ocean
the witness of its own future
a slow crumbling home.

And when this ridge finally arrives
at the edge of the shore, my footsteps with it
all the impermeable weight
that bears down from my head to my heels
will float like a sun at the edge of the world
and find its way to the ocean's bottom
drifting, perhaps, to the place where once
these sensations took root.

2

I am the father of four children,
three of them living.
It is a simple mathematics.
One plus one, minus one, plus two.

I have touched loss
and I have touched grief
but not at the hands of another.

I do not pretend all things are equal.

3

Washed ashore
each bulb of kelp an orb of possibility
fragile in the hands of a man
but able to travel distances none could imagine sustaining
from the tendons & muscles of their bodies.

Loss is a thing we often attribute to the heart
but what of the floating loss of salt & kelp, adrift,
made material in the gelatinous space of
sea & earth
floating like the silent breath of a child unreturned
to this earth.

Floating like the spirit of a child
made manifest beyond our tangible understanding.

4

She is not like the journey of a river to sea,
nor like the way a redwood punctures heaven.

She is something else.

Something not unspeakable
but unknown in this form.

A thing once held

no longer
as I stand on this edge
the end of the beginning.

2

COASTAL
after Romare Bearden

1

The interest is in
the pull of desire.

The way a pelican hovers
for a moment
before her dive.

A rush of wind
and then, the plunge.

In the paragon waters
sunlit sustenance in the glossy scales.

And the gray yearning
an instance of music
and the silent reverberations
of the seal's paddle.

Risen, again, belly full
to sail the sky above this ocean.

If only men could understand
this ease

to resist their currency
in the murkiness of water

wear their calico
with loose understanding.

2

Every wind that enters
this coast
is a moment for want
to redefine itself
and make its home
with lingering.

And on the shore
the women sing, praise and lament
pray the tide will bury the empty-bellied vessels
to make their bows a home for sharks and plankton

to pull ashore the hulls of flesh and blood
rest them weary by the cook-pot
nourish them to remember their names.

They call to the pelican above
to steer the mast to forgotten horizons
to lead these matelots to a home of their own.
A place, perhaps just soft enough
that they will discover a love, however small
to keep them from stealing another's.

SUCCESSION

The rough ends of a cut grass
      floating in an uneven sky.

The sun is a dim-lit fire
      extinguishing the peaks of the day.

As the black begins to enter the
      cracks of the city

men face down their ghosts
      in corridors made for shelter.

I am an adherent to my own demise
      each time I distance myself

from the call of the thrush.
      A reminder always of the interspersal

the aural sounds of daylight,
      the shale flaking at the cracks of our feet.

Summoning a pale blue buoy between earth and shore
      to live with what we cannot know.

When dawn arrives, the thick fog of the bay lingering in the long grasses,
      and again, we begin.

What does it mean then,
this redefining of oneself?

A man standing at the shore can only see so much expanse
before he sees himself.

Mist and scent fill the air
like a prayer rising to the ears of God

and the thickness of the sea swallows both tongue and sight.

LOCAL

Winter lingers on the valley floor,
mist rising in its own essence.

We are reminded of the solitary ways we interpret loss
the temporal flash of an old thatch roof
the hands that made a place for us.

A felled tree becomes a home
made of its surroundings
local, in the way our own skin might be.

The markings of a mask,
etched less with a tool
and more the steady hands of a man,
a pattern shaped in the old order,
a scar on the tree
intended to mark a life.

CANTO FOR PASADENA

Carved in the heart of a valley
I close my eyes to the dissipating asphalt
and imagine a river running south.

Sinking in a sea of syllables
we seek refuge on tree-palmed streets.

At the mouth of the arroyo seco
a roar of rockets
shaping a vision from earth to space
the dream of Pasadena to orbit the earth
to witness the topography from on high.

Like the archangel San Gabriel
floating above this place
the clouds shifting atop a peak
standing in a valley of blue, we gaze up
shaded by the songs of jacaranda and pepper trees
brick and stone
the bougainvillea vines winding through cracks.

There is a calmness here
the hum of the highway
and the ancient river sound.

If you open your eyes just right
the midday sun will show you the desert
will reveal the oasis surrounding you.

If you close your eyes and heave your body toward earth
you will hear the ocean, understand the ancient plant life
feel its presence like coral reef.

The hummingbird drinks from the bottlebrush
and floats in space like a countryless man
finds its route on an earthen byway
and understands migration's song.

We are not like the hummingbird,
fixated on our odd constructions
unable to decipher root from leaf.

But somehow this valley sustains us
no matter how we've worked for erasure
the river gurgles in laughter
and every street sprouts something new
life unstopped by borders
concrete or otherwise.

IN THE "POST-CONFLICT" NATION

Not like the navigator
who felt his hair for wind
& let the sail free,

he rises each day to the incessant
the constant reminder as his feet touch earth
that this was once his own
was once the bracket that held plow & spade
that fed his nation.

And the travelers along the silk road
knew this valley was more than fulfillment
more than a man could ask.

But in this age of separation
from land & plow
he returns from afar
only to wander slowly
only to watch his children
piece string and dye for a coin.

Blind drifting
in the land of his ancestors
he becomes a daily witness.

Foreign-steppers
intent on reviving history
every history but their own.

His parched throat mutters the byword
praise not the living
nor their hunger.

If only his child were an artifact
were something worthy of care and protection,

if only water sprang from rubble
in abundance could they drink.

If only his child were an artifact
broken like a statue.

OUR RETURNING

We've come this far
only to find that what we've known
no one cares to remember.

Not the murder of the Coptic monk in Texas
vanished & abandoned in some backwoods marsh.

Not the priest who collected his bones
wrapped & buried them where rivers once ran.

Not the deaths of the campesinos
blood lingering in the furrows of our lettuce.

Not the children who stitch their dreams
in the pockets of our clothing.

We have forgotten our own names
only to be reminded by the echoes in the canyon.

The way of the earth
is to wither and return to itself
and we too will go this way.
But we are not like the earth,
we will not return to ourselves.
Perhaps we return inside memory
to a time before ourselves.

We have been granted a map to the headwaters
if only we can learn to read & wade
read & wade.

SONG OF THE DISPERSED

Who put the hammer and the hoe in the hands of the poor?
—Third World, "Freedom Song"

And there was a moment when things began to break.

Even the cracked earth bears water.

But that moment was not enough
has never served as salve for chafed hands

and not because we are greedy
but because we are here
because we have been here
toiling

not for recognition
but survival.

When all of the bounty comes from another land
even the seed knows no home.

And the heart of a cancerous man
shrinks oceans
just as the ringing ear of a child
finds music in the sky.

And we continue our labor, knowing
that in the sordid steps of history
the staircase plays favorites.

And they talk and talk and talk
but we know for the verbose
even the river creates anxiety

just as when the rain falls
the thickness of the clouds is an illusion.

Just as on the ringed finger of a man
all possibility is enshrined.

And if our tongues were made of silt
nothing would die when we speak.

And if each of us were named for possibility
the earth would harbor less cement.

The axle of history
greased by blood and amazement

and the power of memory
existing in the history of death.

Death, the resurrection
of memory.

But we know virtually nothing of this history
only that it makes us whole.

THAW

Nothing from this moment can be complete
a grain in the field of want.

A bird sings only to know her song
to feel the weight of a branch vibrating beneath her claws.

Isis gathered the bones of her murdered brother and we recall those days,
power manifest in knowledge.

And in this city, there is a river in the midst of a building,
its glass fractured by the tension of star & sky.

The woman inside feels knifing glances
from the men inside.

The sidewalk speckled with hope and numbness.

The tree out front makes an attempt for sky
but it cannot puncture the firmament.

There is a frost coming
appointed to permeate the surfaces,
make for slick and difficult passage.

The women steadfast in their knowing
will step through it.

The men will wait
for the thaw.

WORK

Chained to an ancient idea
she took the tool into her hand
and began her meticulous labor.

To shape a thing
according to the colors
in one's head.

We give without asking
for return.

The way a mother might
braid her child's hair
thinking of vines,
of her childhood home,
the plant she can no longer name.

And like plow to earth
a mouth full of singing
and the bird floating in the tree
eyes fixed on the pistil of the bloom.

She can see the way the bird
looks sharply
the way her own body
sinks into the earth
with a certain kind of pain
as if the soil were made
from fragments of home.

To say that this is timeless
is not to understand
the way time is both fixed
and ever-present.

She is a mirror of herself
hunched in a furrow of forgetfulness
traded on the land by sweat and burn.

Forget me, she says,
forget that my body ever rose on this earth.
But the bird in the tree keeps peering,
keeps seeing,
keeps tipping its wings

As if there and here
were always the same,
as if one blanket could cover
the beds of millions.

WHO FEELS IT, KNOWS IT
after Amiri Baraka

This one's for the children
who'll learn to steer their hearts
in the direction farthest from this shore
to the land where we place our names

sinking in a sea of syllables
we seek refuge from torture
within torture
and get denied
political asylum from political bombast
doors open in taunt
guided by the cultureless
the ones who think the world is new

Rebel music

assassinated

Rebel music

truth of history
is the truth of humanity
singing on the rock of reality
stranded in the streets

and what if we were told
that everything we've seen
the bones of the shattered
the veins bursting in air
the lives torn between rib cage
and small intestine

were never seen at all?

Rebel music

mutilated

Rebel music

and what if we were told
that all the foods we've touched

forged in the soil of our wrists
tilled in the creases of our feet
have never been tasted?

burial in the burial of the
living dead

discovering
in the discovery of the tainted

stolen bones in the museum
of Shatan

Rebel music

mangled

Rebel music

trade the world
in your world trade
structural violence
in your structural adjustment
shift yourself
make the world think you something good

Rebel music

conquered

Rebel music

singing from the skin
stinging from the skin
think yourself more powerful than the sea
than the bones in the sea

Rebel music

crushing

Rebel music

take it back to the people
who still have faith in Columbus
& his shipwrecked fools

who has more power in the eyes
of the Truth
the one who can speak across oceans
or the one who taints the tide?

sail on the efficacy ship
our voices carry in any wind that blows

Rebel music

risin' up

Rebel music

in the world of the living
it is known that the elders
ain't past
they are present
vivid as genocide

Rebel music

catapulting

Rebel music

lick the fire
and burn your tongue
fireword
fireword
fire-
word!

WILD

"Wild for life" as Lorde once said,
our futures broken
like the bones of lessons.

A prayer for the right kind of mending
a limp only noticeable in memory.

We are wild like this.

Wild in our ways of knowing.

Wild in the sandstorm of a forgotten sea.

Wild in the blooming on our kitchen tables.

Wild from the onset of winter.

Wild in our desire for flight.

Wild for life
until we tame and tame
dam the rivers of our freedom.

Wild for life
the way the wind hollows our lungs
gives us room for more.

Wild for life
even when dragged by the
trudging mud of memory.

Wild for life
the way our food once was,
sustenance from old ways.

Wild like the song
that makes us whole again.

Wild like this.

Wild like the spidered patterns of the coral reef.

Wild like the infinite crevices that shape our way.

Wild like the water we breathe.

UNKNOWING

What might it mean to live
where we do not create sorrow
where our gathering can be magnified?

A formidable perch.
A simulacrum of grace.
A remembrance.

Striving for a shadow of something otherworldly
a handful of salt eroding stone.

Are we content in our final knowing,
our steady-handed assurances
uttered so confidently, even as our eyes betray us?

There is a space between knowing and not knowing
that defines each of our lives.

When I was a child my grandmother kept rabbits
in a small green shed.
In the settling district of Cairo
they made a life of that small place.

My other grandmother,
up in the green of the Nile Delta,
kept chickens on the roof of her apartment building.

Both made their way to our kitchen tables
filling the basin of my unknowing.

GLIMPSE

From the road we see a flash of it
caught somewhere between the stretching leaves & boughs
and the gray damp horizon.

Movement and muscle to be sure
the mystery of realization
slowing down the spin of earth.

It was a site unseen in the tall grass
like water easing through braided fingers
a remnant, allusive and thin.

The children, silent for a change
tracing shadows with their eyes
and a whisper too faint to hear

bounce and sway,
the soft sponge of earth
enshrining history in the steps they take.

Everything we think we see
becomes a harbinger of memory
freed by the distance of space.

And suddenly you are aware
that the place you step
is no place of your own,

the albatross of empire long taken flight
as we reside beneath the shade
of her wings.

And how then do we thrive
in this,
this long-divided place?

A constant recollection of our own skin
freeing us
with the crack of remembrance.

And the child quietly mutters,
as the acorns drop to the ground
their echo a presence

like the split trunk before us
a reminder of the storms
that move through here.

SEEING

How did the world
collapse itself
into this?

A soft canopy shading both
sun and history
in a way only solace must.

I have found myself
in the shadow of the cliffs
the permeating change of the watershed

reminded here only of the aqua salt of sea and
the wholesale charge of a city, miles from here
ever-present in the soil of memory.

I lose myself in the confluence of words
in the calligraphic seeing of time
once and always at once.

I have come to learn
always at the edge of something
that poetry is not sacred
the sacred is sacred

but the words may lead us there
if only for a moment
asking of us something more than speech.

Perhaps it is there that we begin to understand
the meaning of things
the way a man's hands wrench

the neck of a stranger
how his feet kick the legs out
from under him

leaving the weight of his body in the mercy of overkill.
I am reminded of a woman in grief
her son divided by land, by triggers and blood.

There were the hands of another,
who slid inside her palm
an envelope, and whispered,

go and bring him.
They carried him over, tucked him under
hid him inside

sheltered him closely.
But the men of sordid allegiance
with their eyes made of convex lenses

polycarbonate searing,
spotted him like a laser
searching for night.

They placed him in a cage made of polished earth
sent him as far from his heart as they could.
And so the world, then, collapses in on itself

trades our words and memories
for a collision of seeing
and a desperate desire to act.

REFUGE

Somewhere on an island
people chanting
while a man looks back for answers.

His words are written
in stackable blocks
spoken only in night.

His breath is long like his body
always fixed in time
lost in the shadow of itself.

He knows community is plausible
he feels its embrace
he sees it from his window.

But his is an African lament
riddled with aging flowers
waiting for a wayward bloom.

The petals fall inside themselves
like magnificent gazelles
open to a dune horizon.

Their quiet descent, a trail,
like pollen on his fingertips
a colored reminiscence.

The insistence on memory
drives him to the forked river of his childhood
the spring blooms awakened.

The echo of the chant catches his ear
and pulls him back into the room.
This room.

They have all traveled distances
from those waters
and now, here
a foreign sound on this land.

But they have found a place to gather
as the cymbals crash
while he hears this ancient telling.

This thing that pulls him back
And fells him forward like a tree
familiar, perhaps, to those beside him.

Those who come, too,
from the forked river
whose misty banks rise through them.

We are nothing more
than a collection of things remembered
a chant to bring us home.

AN AFTERNOON IN JULY

Thunder cracks open the July afternoon
like the throat of a frightened child.

Tethered stars let loose to a crackling sky.

The wet drooping of the fried-egg tree
bowing in a sheltering
silence from another American terror.

A birdless sky flooding the hope
they love so much to speak of
drowning the Blackness of day,
sheets of rain blurring our vision.

We can almost see another way
the parable of the dead
and the green shoots of life.

We tack the perforated edges of history to our fading memories
while imagining nation in a false light.

One neighbor waves from the car,
the other from the porch,
they do not know one another.

I cannot speak to a healing steeped in fictional possibility
but I can speak of a calculation
laid bare by the entrails of history.

The rain pounds harder
and the water breaks free
the veins of the leaves rushing to a nearby stem.

An unmoored boat pushed by the stirring swells
an odd and bitter nourishment in the wake of the dead.

What does America mean to you?
Either I am not you, or there is no meaning.

The question itself another torrent.

And the flapping of flags;
the blood, cold, and ocean/sky.

We are drowning in that ocean
reaching for the sky.

And they claim their freedom so freely
while those who died by them,
die again.

ROCK HEAD
after David Hammons & for Simone Leigh

When I saw it first, up close
it was the hands of a woman
that placed it there
a vision in the context of my own past
a bridge made evident
by those made to wander.

Of course she would recognize kin,
her, the maker of faces
the sculptor of eyeless sight.

There was something about the ancients,
trinitarian
the rockstone
excavated from some waters
reminiscent of the river

the hairs from the heads
young and old
brothers curled in their own simple semblance
a twist as old as breath, we are sure,
no matter the street or desert.

But there beside the faces of Fayoum,
the place of my mother
and the countenance of my father
a marker for amalgamation.

That Kushite bald patch
on the crown of remembrance
a crack to the dome
where wisdom seeps.

I felt the whole of history
breeze through that crack
shaping the tools
that shape the faces
that rock the head
and cause us
to see.

THE UNLEARNING
for Kwame Dawes

> *And if we should live up in the hills.*
> —Burning Spear

Death comes to us,
a shadow of itself.

Death, at the hands of the state.
Death, so often.
Death, so African.
Death, ancestry.
Black death.

A death that does not happen
in a foreign language.

Babylon system.
      Vampire.
Wrapping its growing hands
around the larynx of a man.

        But Babylon cannot have our children.

Babylon cannot conqueror bond,
cannot take the memory from a mother
or the sting from a father.

Oh Obadiah Obadiah
*Jah Jah sent us to catch vampire.**

An incantation sung for the marauders.

A trail that leads to warmth.
A synesthetic in the bush.
A man up in the hills.

A prism in the wings of a hummingbird
ruby-throated
a flash to carry the moment
a reminder of the fleeting colors
inhabiting our lives.

So we find a place of stillness
hold our staff like the flag of tomorrow
and chant:

And if we should live up in the hills

And in these hills
the unlearning.
The maroon.
The marronage from senseless death.

Another century
& it remains the same.

The man in the hills
his head to the ground
hears the reverberations
from the whale at sea.

Her sonic song rippling from
ocean to shore
to the center of this volcanic mass.

Up through the earth,
this earth,
a reminder that the journey to the hills
has always been a journey from death.

Lyrics from Ketch Vampire written by Devon Irons, music by Lee Scratch Perry

REVELATION: AFRICA: DIASPORA

It is less about the opaqueness of the sky
and more the subtle alluvion of snowfall.

We are reminded that the past is as near
as memory.

The ox yoke always a twinning
a mirror of itself.

The thundering voice
of unraveling

a full-body exaltation
salted with the dust of earth.

We have been made to shrink
to shed our circumstances for an idea.

The corporeal marketed in a way unimaginable
the mind affixed in its own terrarium.

When the four incorporeal creatures
make their way to this earth

the lion, the calf, the man, and the eagle
how do they decipher beast from human?

"Who was, and is, and is to come"
we take our chance at seeing again.

From horizon to seashore
the earth tilts on high

magnifying its glory
and bringing us to our feet.

We chant in the order of Melchizedek.
We watch the islands recede.

We call upon the Spirit
and sing our way back home.

ACKNOWLEDGMENTS

I want to thank the editors of the following journals where several of these poems initially appeared: *Academy of American Poets' Poem-a-Day*, *Anomaly Magazine*, *Columbia Poetry Review*, *The Fight & The Fiddle*, *Indiana Review*, *Mizna*, *Prairie Schooner*, *Vassar Review*, *Washington Square Review*, *World Literature Today*, and the *Yale Review*. And also the editors of the anthologies *Bearden's Odyssey: Poets Respond to the Art of Romare Bearden*, *Fractured Ecologies*, and *The Mighty Stream: Poems in Celebration of Martin Luther King*. My deepest gratitude and thanks to dancer and choreographer Onye Ozuzu for incorporating my poem "Work" into the performance and installation of her brilliant piece, *Project Tool*.

To my African Poetry Book Fund colleagues: Chris Abani, Gabeba Baderoon, Kwame Dawes, Bernardine Evaristo, Aracelis Girmay, John Keene, and Phillippa Yaa de Villiers, who always remind me what it means to be a part of a borderless community. To Emanuel Admassu, Patricia Barbeito, Ilene Chaiken, Ama Codjoe, Tjawangwa Dema, Tony Johnson, Douglas Kearney, John Murillo, John-Carlos Perea, Nicole Sealey, Mahtem Shifferaw, Tavares Strachan, and Stanley Wolukau-Wanambwa for the rock steady.

To my dear editor Parneshia Jones, always building and forward-looking, and the whole crew at Northwestern University Press for their tireless and necessary work.

Finally, my unending love to my family, my beloved Coptic community worldwide, and all the elders, co-conspirators, inspirators, and dear friends—too many to name—who have helped me shape a full and consequential life. Give thanks!